THE *BEST ADVICE* IN SIX WORDS

Also by Larry Smith

The
BEST
ADVICE
in **SIX** Words

Writers Famous and Obscure on
Love, Sex, Money, Friendship,
Family, Work, and Much More

from SMITH Magazine
edited by **Larry Smith**
with Shauna Greene

 St. Martin's Griffin ♨ New York

www.stmartins.com

Designed by Jonathan Bennett & Phil Mazzone

Library of Congress Cataloging-in-Publication Data

The best advice in six words : writers famous and obscure on love, sex, money,
friendship, family, work, and much more / Larry Smith.—First edition.
      p. cm
   ISBN 978-1-250-06701-2 (hardcover)
   ISBN 978-1-4668-7493-0 (e-book)
  1. Life—Quotations, maxims, etc. 2. Conduct of life—Quotations, maxims, etc.
3. Life—Humor. 4. Conduct of life—Humor. 5. Quotations, English. I. Smith,
Larry, 1968– compiler. II. Title: Writers famous and obscure on love, sex, money,
friendship, family, work, and much more.
   PN6084.L53B47 2015
   818'.60208—dc23

                                                              2015019392

Our books may be purchased for promotional, educational, or business use.
Please contact your local bookseller or the Macmillan Corporate and
Premium Sales Department at (800) 221-7945, extension 5442, or by e-mail
at MacmillanSpecialMarkets@macmillan.com.

First Edition: November 2015

10 9 8 7 6 5 4 3 2 1

Preface

1,000 Pieces of Advice, Six Words at a Time

I can't get enough good advice. As a kid, I loved hearing old-timey wisdom from my grandparents. Now, I've never met a graduation speech I didn't love, am a sucker for a promising magazine cover line at the newsstand, and listen to way too many TED talks. And as someone who's spent most of the last decade asking people to be succinct, I appreciate thoughts that get right to the point, advice such as "Reading makes you a better writer," "Your greatest weapon is your wit," and "Stumbling looks like a dance eventually."

Besides being good advice, the above examples have one thing in common: they are six words. Since 2006, I've been asking people to sum up their lives in exactly six words on the storytelling community

I founded, Six Words from SMITH Magazine. We call these short life stories "Six-Word Memoirs," a personal twist on the form that, according to literary lore, Hemingway started when challenged in a bar to write a whole novel in just six words ("For sale: baby shoes, never worn.").

The Six-Word Memoir® project has since taken on a life beyond my wildest dreams. Nine years and more than one million stories later, the six-word concept has become a bestselling book series and board game, a teaching tool used across the world, and a powerful way to spur on self-expression for anyone and everyone. Preachers and rabbis have embraced six-word prayers as a way to distill faith. In hospitals and veterans' groups, after-school programs, around dinner tables, and (naturally) during speed dates, the six-word form has been used to foster understanding, ease communication, and break the ice.

The six-word constraint forces us to figure out the essence of who we are and what matters most—and works especially well when doling out advice.

From the silly ("Don't pee on an electric fence.") to the profound

("Be the someone they can call.") to the obvious notions that we all occasionally need to recall ("Your phone does not love you.") there's a lot of wisdom in these six-word morsels.

And there are a lot of morsels. The 1,000 contributions found here are just a fraction of the six-word submissions we received. (The strict grammarians among us will notice that the occasional offering pushes the limits of what is exactly "six," but we decided to be open-minded and count contractions and hyphenations as one word.)

As is true of all our six-word books, this one is a mix of contributions from the famous and the unknown. Several six worders come from some of our favorite writers, such as Elizabeth Gilbert who reminds us that "Chances are, your editor is right," David Baldacci who suggests, "Can't say something nice? Try fiction," and Jodi Picoult, who implores us: "Don't set your brother on fire." We're delighted to offer essential wisdom from Whoopi Goldberg, Julianne Moore, Mario Batali, Madeleine Albright, Maria Shriver, and others from the worlds of film, music, food, finance, comedy, wellness, and academia. This book features a half-dozen well-chosen words from a

Poet Laureate, Oscar, Emmy, and Tony winners, a couple of Mac-Arthur Genius recipients, and even a few of our favorite professional advice columnists.

I always learn so much from others when we put the call out for a new six-word challenge. As I scrolled through the many, many submissions on SixWordMemoirs.com, I recalled a concept called "the network effect" that says the value of something grows in relation to others who use it. That's very much true in the six-word world. With each story, our project becomes bigger, stronger, and more interesting. With that in mind, I hope you too will share your six-word advice or six words on any part of your life at SixWordMemoirs.com.

—Larry Smith
Founder, Six Words from SMITH Magazine

THE *BEST ADVICE* IN SIX WORDS

Be an optimist who worries often.

—SECRETARY OF STATE MADELEINE ALBRIGHT

Enthusiasm **opens more doors than pessimism.**

—JOHN THORNTON

Basic needs: backbone, wishbone, funny bone.

—RAVEN OKEEFE

For a minute, laughter cures everything.

—KEN STASIAK

When in doubt, channel **Dolly Parton.**

—ALLISON GLOCK

Every experience is another college essay.

—RUBY REILLY

Trust me: Kiss every nationality possible.

—TWANNA A. HINES

Simplify your life.
Amplify your pleasure.

—JANA BEATTIE EGGERS

Free cheese only comes in traps.

—ED BOLAND

Close the blinds. Dance around naked!

—ERIN SCUSSEL

BOLD TRUTH
trumps all cards dealt.
—DOTTIE BOWMAN

Bankruptcy,

suicide,

jackpot:

ordered by probability.

—JOSH AXELRAD

Nobody really needs a *BILLION* dollars.

—CRAIG NEWMARK

Stop listening to the irrational thoughts.

—JEN EVANS

Brotherhood, having someone's back through **HELL***.*

—CLAYTON JOHNSTON

Ice cream: dish best served cold.

—RONNY PASCALE

Panic is more dangerous than **Ebola**.

—DR. ANDREW ROZMIAREK

Never forget where you came from!

—DANIELLE BROOKS

A heartfelt apology resolves most conflicts.

—AYELET WALDMAN

Don't wait
to appreciate your beauty.

—LAURIE FURBER

Always **create** more than you **destroy**.

—MADDY SCHNEIDER

Start off your day with sex.

—NANCY LEVENSON

Do not search symptoms on WebMD.

—DANIELLE BITNER

Just make something every single day.

—NOAH SCALIN

Live, write, dream, all at once.

—ALAN CHEUSE

Dreams don't work **unless you do**.

— BRANDI VAISEY MARSEY

Find freedom in a little *HEDONISM.*

—TONYA MILLER

Sometimes on low,
others on **high**.

—MARIO BATALI

Leave a little for the imagination.

—*GUY AUSTIN*

When in doubt, turn heat down.

—*DAVID SAX*

Always wear pants when you cook.

—*HUGH WEBER*

Throw a stranger an unexpected smile.

—*RACHEL FETRIDGE*

Breathe one syllable at a time.

—*TINA CHANG*

No more writing without getting paid.

—*GRAYDON CARTER*

100 headlines for one good one.

—*KIRK CITRON*

Put pen to paper every day.

—*LISA BROWN*

Write daily. Submit often.
            Get published.

—*DONNA REEVE*

No talking until I say so.

—DONI WILSON

Take time to spread global peace.

—MARC BEKOFF

Hope, it's the last to die.

—CHRIS GROSSO

Listen to the underground radio station.

—EDWIN SMALL

Wake at first light; enjoy quiet.

—JOHN CARNETT

Enjoy the way. Commute by bike.

—JAMES CRAIG WALLEN

Home for family dinner whenever possible.

—LILLA GOURLEY

Make **magic** at your kitchen table.

—COLEEN GOODSON

Happiness: marry for sex, not money.

—NICOLE BELAND

Marry an orphan. No family drama.

—HEATHER BRAXTON

Live far away from your in-laws.

—JENNY MOLLEN

"Do I look fat?" "NO, HONEY."

—JASON BIGGS

Look into each other's eyes daily.

—LYNN MISKELL

I finally know: skinnier isn't happier.

—LIZZIE LEE

Don't waste what others desperately seek.

—SARITA ALSTON

Turn off water when brushing teeth.

—SARA MANEWITH

Use contraception. Slow reproduction. Go vegetarian.

—CAROLINE HALE

Don't put that in your mouth.

—MORGAN SPURLOCK

Develop an insatiable appetite for feedback.

—KEN GOLDBERG

Don't stop to argue with critics.

—COLLEEN DOLAN STOVER

Ignore your critics, unless they're right.

—JEFF TIEDRICH

Don't fight for what others believe.

—AUSTYN YARRINGTON

TRUTH doesn't rely on being believed.

—DINA HILLIER

Everything's possible: We're made of miracles.

—VAN JONES

Take two and hit to right.

—GLEN WAGGONER

Breathe in. Breathe out. Or die.

—KARI HARENDORF

When thrown a strike, don't bunt.

—JOHANNA McCHESNEY

Always say no to the Jägerbombs.

—DEBBIE McKEOWN

Sometimes not giving is the gift.

—KATE FAL

Appreciating creates more joy than acquiring.

—ALEXIS DAVIDSON

Don't publish books about saving trees.

—EMILY R. DOLL

There's something therapeutic in vacuuming floors.

—ARLENE PESIGAN

You only have to convince yourself.

—EDDIE HUANG

Poor starts don't guarantee poor finishes.

—DUSTIN DOYLE

Education breaks the cycle of poverty.

—GEOFFREY CANADA

Bring a problem. Bring a resolution.

—*DONNA HAMILTON*

Help others succeed. It is addictive.

—*SAM DAVIS*

Don't **allow** disability to stop you.

—*STEPHANIE TORRENO*

Not getting everything makes you stronger.

—*SABA SULAIMAN*

There is strength in being vulnerable.

—*STEVEN BERKOWITZ*

Fall down five, get up six.

—*MICHAEL CONNELLY*

Choose your words and indulgences wisely.

—*SHAUNA HEALY GREENE*

When the liver says stop, listen.

—*NAN WIGINGTON*

Do not ignore stone in shoe.

—*MICHELLE SYDNEY LEVY BLAUSTEIN*

Assume everyone is driving with kids.

—*TIM BARKOW*

Fake it 'til you become it.

—*AMY CUDDY*

Good posture trumps insecurity every time.

—*SUSANNE KUZNETSKY*

Slouching creates sadness. Sit up straight.

—RINATTA PARIES

It's all body language, walk tall.

—ASHLEY AHN

There's always time to reinvent yourself.

—KATHRYN BUDIG

Take the epidural. And the fentanyl.

—AMY L. KEYISHIAN

"Because I'm your mother. **That's why.**"

—DARRYL FORMAN

Don't just itch it, wash it.

—MICHELE MOZELSIO

It's never too late to play.

—*GLEN KEITH DeMERITT*

Blind dates don't need guide dogs.

—*ADRIANO MORAES*

Hope is not an investment strategy.

—*JEAN CHATZKY*

Save more, spend less, avoid ripoffs.

—*CLARK HOWARD*

Buy low. Sell high. (Both infrequently.)

—*GARY BELSKY*

Wink at teller when depositing singles.

—*LILY BURANA*

Life story: write now, pay later.

—*NATALIE D-NAPOLEON*

Happiness: subtract meaningless work from life.

—*ANNA GRIFFIN*

Slightly underpaid better than vastly overworked.

—*BRENT PERDUE*

Exhale a nightmare, inhale a possibility.

—*MARTY BLACKMER*

Carpal tunnel ain't worth the royalties.

—*SHANE DAVIS*

When in doubt? Write it out.

—*BAMBIE WODKINS*

Freedom is the prize. Not money.

—*BRANDI S. GORDON*

Twenty wooden nickels: **one wooden dollar**.

—*BILLY COLLINS*

Crime pays but freedom is better.

—*JUDGE ALEX FERRER*

Cut the babble! Just dance. Dabble.

—*JOE LOYA*

Peddle your oddities
as precious commodities.

—*SINEAD McKEOUGH*

Just believe in yourself, you idiot.

—*DANA EAGLE*

Trust me, you're not that funny.

—*KYLE GORDON*

Big heads weigh your life down.

—*RUTH F. HUNT*

Son, never believe your own clippings.

—*LONNIE BUNCH*

Work every angle, don't cut corners.

—*VICKI BOWEN HEWES*

You can't brag about being humble.

—*KAITLYN MONKEMEYER*

Wanting less feels like getting more.

—*TANYA ARTERBURN*

The calculator is not always right.

—*JIMMY WHITE*

There is *always* room to moonwalk.

—ABBY SHER

Never leave home for a boy.

—AMBER DERMONT

Don't lose yourself in his shadow.

—SUZANNE S. AUSTIN-HILL

No man is worth 300 sandwiches.

—KAT BRADY

Happy marriage? Tease each other constantly.

—SIMON DOONAN

Two times a week (at least).

−JOE KRISHNAN

Passionate arguments lead to passionate sex.

−TONI ESPERANZA CHADWELL

Hug with meaning. Kiss with tongue.

−KATIE KRENTZ

Secret to happy marriage:
            separate bathrooms.

−MARY McCONNELL

Art doesn't care about color, sex.

—*WHOOPI GOLDBERG*

It's how—not who—you love.

—*DEB PUCHALLA*

Go beyond the slogans and rhetoric.

—*PEDRO NOGUERA*

Never volunteer to fight The Mountain.

—*PANIO GIANOPOULOS*

Mountains won't move, but stones will.

—*JESSICA GARDNER*

Powerful avalanches begin with small shifts.

—*PAMELA McFARLAND WALSH*

Conquered mountains are above the fog.

—*CHARLES MURRAY*

To get an "A," ask questions.

—*ZAK NELSON*

Never wear shorts on a plane.

—*MIKE KESSLER*

In a hole . . . then stop digging.

—*JESSICA MERYL NAUDZIUNAS*

The opposite of perfection is DONE.

—*MICHAEL MARGOLIS*

Best is the enemy of good.

—*SUSAN MAHAN*

Who cares less runs the relationship.

—*JOHN SIMPSON*

You can always take another step.

—*ALEXIS RYAN*

Saying "I understand" can work wonders.

—*DOUGALD LAMONT*

Most powerful words:
"Thanks" and "Sorry."

—*JENNIFER EGAN*

Speak up:
never know who's listening.
—SEN. KIRSTEN GILLIBRAND

Speak kindly,
someone always hears you.
—ELEANOR SANCHEZ

NO ONE is looking at you.

—TAVI GEVINSON

You're not in high school anymore.

—ADELA GRIFFIN

Temporary circumstances don't equal
permanent reality.

—GREG HARTLE

Change the world by being yourself.

—AMY POEHLER, SMART GIRLS

Don't criticize your teenage daughter's hair.

—*KATE HINDS*

It doesn't matter what *they* think.

—*DANIEL PINK*

Stand for something, not against everything.

—*KATHLEEN FETTERS-LOSSI*

Passion, happiness, balance over everything else.

—*RYAN POTTER*

There is more out there, look.

—*JAMES GLOVER*

Bring your weather to the picnic.

—*HARLAN COBEN*

Cooking and life:
patience and persistence.

—*THOMAS KELLER*

Buy real food,
cook it simply.

—*MARK BITTMAN*

Days are long; years are short.

—GRETCHEN RUBIN

I guarantee you: certainty is impossible.

—A. J. JACOBS

Pretend impossibilities are possible. They are.

—SANDI HEMMERLEIN

Be aware this might not work.

—SOL SHIELDS

A stranger rings, a friend knocks.

—DAVE EGGERS

Old friends will keep you young.

—CAROL SMITH

When you find your tribe, stay.

—MISHELL DeFELICE

College friends will be forever friends.

—AMY WARD

Always stick to your mother-fucking guns!

—TED RHEINGOLD

Never too late to change paths.

—DAVID BOYER

Go where you have been invited.

—JOEL GARLAND

Accept invitations or they'll dry up.

—TOM KATER

Never barter with a snappish waiter.

—SHERRY AINSCOUGH

When snapped at, don't snap back.

—CRYSTA KESSLER

When in doubt, aim for grace.

—PATRICIA RYAN

As like Cary Grant as possible.

—*TIM GUNN*

Confidence and grace: always in style.

—MOLLY O'GORMAN

Look taller wearing tone on tone.

—MICHAELA JEDINAK

Dad said: "Think Yiddish, dress British."

—SCOTT SIMON

How to wear leather pants: don't.

—JUSTIN BONTHUYS

You realize those sunglasses aren't mirrored?

—PHIL OSHVA

Don't poof your hair. Just don't.

—LAUREN SMITH

While cutting hair, never say, "Oops."

—*MOLLY MOBLO PERUSSE*

Slow's faster. Fast is merely exhausting.

—*CHRISTINE LOUISE HOHLBAUM*

A hurried child just slows down.

—*MJ BORRELLI*

Learn to love in slow motion.

—*LOUISE TO*

If they're not laughing, talk faster.

—*LEA DeLARIA*

Your greatest weapon is your wit.

—*HANNAH DeLALLO*

DON'T POST
it on the Internet.

—MOLLY JONG-FAST

DON'T BLAME
it on the Internet.

—COLLIN MACK

Slow is smooth, smooth is fast.

—*RYAN JAMES SITTLER*

When in doubt, it's probably illegal.

—*NATHAN SCOGGINS*

Life is long. Then it isn't.

—*MELINDA KIGER CHEVAL*

Nothing's forever but your momma's love.

—*ALYSON BODAI*

It's show business. Make a show.

—*ROBERTA GALE*

Don't be on time: be early.

—*MICHAEL IAN BLACK*

Overthinking seems to result in **underliving**.

—GAIL URQUHART

Deadlines are there to help you.

—NOL MARTÍN-TUNGPALAN

Geniuses do not work to **deadlines.**

—ANTHONY GRANT GORDON

With great power comes great headaches.

—MELISSA GREEN

Never forget to bring migraine meds.

—ROBERTA KAPLAN

Take worst job at best place.

—ELIOT KAPLAN

Job interviews are great learning places.

—STEVE SCHOHAN

Best lessons come from worst boss.

—LIZ SCHUMAN

Your apartment is the worst office.

—DAN HENRIKSEN

Never, ever drunk dial your boss.

—KAMAL PARBHAKAR

Ladies, lighting is everything after 50.

—MARGIE GORMAN

You can't fix it in post.

—CHRISTY PESSAGNO

Make time for deep delicious sleep.

—VICKI LAGER

Teeth: brushed. Hair: fussed. Sack: trussed.

—CONSTABLE DOOLEY

Endure. Tomorrow is a different day.

—KAREN MUNRO

Get some sleep. Start fresh tomorrow.

—CHRISTY SANTOS

Be a doer, not a dreamer.

—SHONDA RHIMES

Overnight success has never happened overnight.

—CHARLES LONDON

Work ethic, not GPA, determines success.

—BELINDA HERNANDEZ

Learn the ropes before challenging customs.

—PAM GRATER

Do NOT pull your grandpa's finger.

—KELLY McQUAIN

Life is a PRISM OF POSSIBILITY.

—NANCY SHARP

The unexamined life's not worth living. . . .*

—COLUM McCANN

*The overexamined life's hardly much better.

Remember those gone. Toast those here.

—*JOHN EVENSON*

When all else fails,
start running.

—*DEAN KARNAZES*

If it's not hurting, try harder.

—*LAURA BETH RAMSAY*

Write until you can't,
then write.

—*L.B. WILSON*

Find your center and hold it

—*KATE COX*

Fall, get up, smile, keep going.

—JAMES FREY

Never stop seeing yourself with wonder.

—ALEXANDRA ROSAS

Don't take it all so **seriously**.

—MARLENA HENRY

Don't be afraid of karaoke machines.

—COURTNEY K. BAMBRICK

Do your best and don't worry.

—LIZ MULLEN

The word "fuck" is unstoppable, poetic.

—ADAM MANSBACH

Eat with vegetarians, sleep with carnivores.

—JAN ALEXANDER

~~(You)~~ Can't always fuck what you want.

—DAN SAVAGE

Learn to budget and fuck effectively.

—LITSA DREMOUSIS

Separate bank accounts; lots of sex.

—MICHAEL L. WEISSMAN

People first, then money, then things.

—SUZE ORMAN

"Collect people, not things."
—Love, Mom.

—ALLISON HEMMING

You are who you are with.

—MARK CURCIO

You're as mature as you act.

—CHELSEA BARNISKIS

Don't discount someone because of age.

—BELINDA BROCK

You: average of five closest friends.

—TIM FERRIS

It's not always the parents' fault.

-HANNAH MORRISON

Post-adolescent? Then stop blaming your parents.

-MOLLY RINGWALD

Teenagers: your mom really knows best!

-AMANDA LEIGH HARRIS

Unfortunately, you WILL become your parents.

-PATRICK KENNEDY

DON'T SET YOUR BROTHER ON FIRE.

—JODI PICOULT

DON'T CHANGE DIAPERS AT FRIENDS' HOMES.

—BOB LEOPOLDO

DON'T BE AFRAID TO BE HAPPY.

—IRIS DELGADO

In small apartments, clean up daily.

—*RACHELL SUMMERS*

Better an armoire than a closet.

—*CHRISTOPHE POURNY*

Expect the worst, embrace the best.

—*ALI HANNA*

Become **indispensable** in the first year.

—*TRA DAVIS*

Memorize all the two-letter Scrabble words.

—*LAUREATTE LOY*

Fear not,
Live in the now.

—GOLDIE HAWN

Turn off your electronics and focus.

—STEVER ROBBINS

Your phone does not love you.

—SCOTT ALEXANDER

Love thy neighbor as thy iPhone.

—GREG OOSE

Disconnect from things you can't control.

—MICHELLE PEREIRA

We connect better with no Wi-Fi.

—CATHERINE HOIS

It's hard to hate up close.

—KAREEM MORELAND

Friends are always. Family is forever.

—LOGAN JAMES GRAHAM

Family: for people with no friends.

—JILL SOBULE

Love your family, like your work.

—JEFF KINNEY

Creativity with crayons, not first names.

—NIKKI WEINSTEIN

Spend less time sharpening pencils. Write.

—ERIKA LaCARNEY

Make people say your name properly.

—ARIA VELASQUEZ

Change your name to Joe Kelly.

—SAID SAYRAFIEZADEH

Tell your wife you love her.

—JIM SCHACHTER

Never keep a compliment to yourself.

—SAMANTHA HAMMER KADRMAS

Hold your head up high always.

—MARIA SHRIVER

Just do what makes you happy!

—KATHERINE SCHWARZENEGGER

Tell kids you're proud of them.

—ASHLEY ALLEN

Wit and lipstick are both weapons.

—ZARA D. GARCIA-ALVAREZ

Confident women are **always** sexy women.

—LOGAN RUN

*Jump from cliffs.
Wear helmet, lipstick.*

—TIFFANY SHLAIN

Try to avoid heroics in heels.

—JENNIFER PUST

Bake the IT folks a pie.

—MOLLY NORTON

There's always time for another episode.

—*TAYLOR TRIPPE*

Never shave your privates too quickly.

—*MAXINE M. MANNION*

Order pie before they run out.

—*JANE & MICHAEL STERN*

Share your story, change the world.

—*GEORGE TAKEI*

Beware crowd pleasing. Don't lose yourself.

—BARATUNDE THURSTON

Torch your bridges, explore your path.

—JOSEPHINE "JOSHIE" ARMSTED

Let goals, not culture, define you.

—DANN BROWN

Don't fear love at first **flight**.

—ALLISON WILLIAMS

Don't be careful; you'll get hurt.

—VIRGINIA HEFFERNAN

Never trust a damn piano player.

—MYRA LEWIS WILLIAMS

Play the piano until it's fun!

—JIMMY WALES

Big challenges make the hours fly.

—C LYNN BACON

Face your demons, then harness them.

—JEANNETTE WALLS

Sacred within me, sacred all around.

—JENN GROSSO

Mental health days are a necessity.

—JULIE FOSTER

Falling down is just balancing practice.

—RODNEY YEE

Stumbling looks like a dance eventually.

—SHANNON WHISSELL

Always make all financial decisions together.

—DAVID McKNIGHT

Money is neither success nor happiness.

—CLAUDIA BEAR

Beware of women without female friends.

—GILLIAN SEGAL

Don't let them direct your story.

—LUCILLE HU

Learn to love your own company.

—TIFFANY SINGLETON

Smile at old people eating alone.

—SALLY FRIEDMAN

Solitude: different from loneliness; embrace it.

—*NICOLE BATTAGLIA*

There's no greater loneliness than narcissism.

—*MONTY GILMER*

*Make necessary beautiful
and beautiful necessary.*

—*LORENZO MATTOZZI*

**Imperfect souls make for
interesting characters.**

—*TROY WORMAN*

Never, ever, underestimate a quiet woman.

—*NEROLI SCHUTT*

Sometimes the more is not merrier.

—*CAITLYN WOOD*

Never open anything with your teeth.

—*CAROLINE GOLDSTEIN*

Put a hat on that baby!

—*ABBY LAUGHLIN*

Say your prayers. Check the oil.

—*STEF RICCA*

Don't sniff the cork, **just drink**.

—*BILL GEIBLER*

Pray in gratitude, not just need.

—*LESLIE A. LONG*

Eat your broccoli and always floss.

—*"WEIRD AL" YANKOVIC*

Floss your tires; rotate your dentures.

—*GREGORY MAGUIRE*

Food is fuel, movement is life.

—*MATT DELANEY*

Always keep your gas tank full.

—*AMANDA SPEER*

Work hard. Play hard. Laugh. Relax.

—*BRIAN LEHRER*

Clean up as you go along.

—*LISA ROMEO*

The good china is for everyday.

—KATIE SCHRODER BOND

The fork goes on the left.

—ALICE VAUGHAN

Slice bagel on plate, not palm.

—MARK ROSENBLUM

Oregano is not the only spice.

—LAURA ZIGMAN

Note, seed the jalapeños next time.

—BARON SEKIYA

If cooking, put butter on it.

—CAMILA YUMI

When mood dictates food, fat follows.

—ANGIE HOER

Gravy makes **everything** a little better.

—STEVE LEASURE

Fresh seafood on Monday? Be skeptical.

—JIM GLADSTONE

Celery salt will change your life.

—MARGOT THOMSON

Silent auctions and alcohol don't mix.

—LARRY SMITH

Blame it on the double vodkas.

—DEBBIE McKEOWN

At pity party, one drink maximum.

—TRICIA JANOSY

Keep drinking until the kids graduate.

—TAYLOR JOHNSON

Wine is just fermented grape juice.

—LAURA MANIEC

Nothing is ever what it seems.

—PHIL BRONSTEIN

Ignorance and bliss are not friends.

—JILLIAN BLANCHARD

Always beware the thesaurus's
sesquipedalian suggestions.

—SUSAN BOROWITZ

Use fun words:

"accoutrements,"

"perspicacious,"

"cuddlesome."

—JACQUELINE RICE

Don't get locked up while engaged!!

—VANESSA CASTRO

Don't use too many exclamation points!!!

—JAMES N. FREY

Self-deception: a life sentence without parole.

—ROB FRALEY

Bail bondsmen only require 10% down.

—AARON DUNCAN

Don't chase "normal." Follow the love.

—CHRISTOPHER TOLLER

Beard plus high school equals success!

—DALTON LANNAN

Baker's chocolate is **NOT** milk chocolate.

—ERIK PALUMBO

Be particular—in life and love.

—ZELDA SHUTE

Visit Grandma every chance you get.

—JANET L. CAPPIELLO

Handle with care, tumble dry low.

—CONSTANCE ZIMMER

Keep thine bits in thy clothes.

—KURSTIN FINCH GNEHM

Don't twerk on Robin Thicke, honey.

—ANNA GOLDFARB

A tree is just a tree.

—HEATHER HOLLE

There is **always** a new black.

—RACHEL TRIGNANO

Drink water every time you cry.

—BETH SCOTT

Hydrate or die, Mom told me.

—PIERA GELARDI

Ask Tooth Fairy for a raise.

—ALLYSON MORGAN

Decisions, not DNA, determine your destiny.

—*LEE FALIN*

Avoid disappointment. Aim at the floor.

—*EDDIE McNAMARA*

Lust is fleeting. Herpes? Not quite.

—*RURAMAI MUSEKIWA*

Don't play the other guy's game.

—*ALAN BENTON*

In love with love isn't Love.

—*CHRISTINE MACDONALD*

Love, it comes in many faces.

—*LAC SU*

Thou shalt not neglect social media.

—DHRUTI SHAH

Thou shalt not Instagram every meal.

—KRISTIN CISZESKI

Engage with those you love offline.

—LISA WURTELE

Texts with Dad: now is **BEAUTIFUL**.

—KATE REIL

No phones on the first date.

—CAMERON VEST

Shower her with expensive jewelry **occasionally**.

—ERIC GRAVINK

Never forget to date your wife.

—*JAMES CRANE-BAKER*

Complaint is poverty, gratitude is riches.

—*CLARA MAI YAN*

Always do more than the minimum.

—*SUZANNE M. RIVERA*

Keep the whining to a minimum.

—*SHAYNA SMILOVITZ*

Go 24 hours without complaining once.

—*MAGGIE PATTON*

Motivation is like underwear: change daily.

—*JESS YOUNG*

Thou shalt cite all thy sources.

—*JIM PRALL*

"Busy" means nothing,
"productive" means **everything**.

—*JULIA JESTER*

Be the fountain, not the drain.

—*JONATHAN VAN METER*

Honesty damages but lies can destroy.

—*KYLYNNE HOLTZ*

Eyes prove lies that mouths say.

—*FAITH HELEN*

Don't do anything I would do.

—*DAVID ULIN*

A liar? You can just tell.

—HON. VICTOR FRIEDMAN

Stay calm, urgent things remain urgent.

—SYLVIA APFELBAUM

Sample the buffet with focused intensity.

—TIM HOYT

The journey: more fun than success.

—RICHARD KIND

Take a breather, help someone else.

—ANDREA WHITE

Laugh at yourself and each other.

—*ELANA FATE*

Happiness: someone to spend Sundays with.

—*KIMBERLY ROSE*

Use your imagination, ignore the hesitation.

—*MARTIN RING*

Find yourself by occasionally getting lost.

—*M. JOHN BURNS*

Bad moods make for good songs.

—*CHRISTIE BECKWITH*

Music heals wounds, soothes battle scars.

—*BRIANNA ROSE ROBINSON*

Country music is a mighty medicine.

—MARTY STUART

Play vinyl. Dance in the dark.

—LESLEY-ANNE EVANS

Let live music be your church.

—KEIRSTEN ALEXANDER

Cut out what's not a guitar.

—WAYNE HENDERSON

Always keep the bathroom door closed.

—ROBERT WOLF

Keep bedroom farts to a minimum. . . .

—SAM HILL

For future reference, start Propecia earlier.

—ADAM ROTH

You can look, but don't touch.

—GREG L. BERRY

Give the cat whatever it wants.

—VICTORIA PALMER

Animals are the **perfect** secret keepers.

—CHELSEY WELLZ

Words are silver, silence is gold.

—AMY DAVERIES

Does it need to be said?

—JULIANNE MOORE

Coming out? Prepare for the worst.

—*BETH GREENFIELD*

Hearts will break. Hugs will mend.

—*MARY SIKKEL*

Even grouches have hearts. Be kind.

—*AUDRA KERR BROWN*

Better to be kind than right.

—*APRIL BAUR DAVIS*

Heavy on praise, light on slights.

—*SHARON HARRIS*

Don't run from, run to something.

—JENNIFER BLANCK

Courage is never doubting your choices.

—*ABBYGAIL DeKRAAI*

Grit your teeth, do your homework.

—*ALLIE CAMPBELL*

Improve the repetitions
until mastery materializes.

—*TSHEPHO BARAKANYE*

Be more awesome than last year.

—*SHILPA SHARMA*

Seeking happiness? The key is travel.

—*ALLISON DALENA*

When in Ireland, carry a raincoat.

—*JACQUELINE MILLER*

Make sure your passport is current.

—LISA HARTE

Three girls, one bathroom.
Bad idea.

—AMY SCHMUCKER

Smart is more sexy than sexy.

—ADRIENNE LADD

Never go to bed wearing makeup.

—AMY HAIR

It always looks better after mascara.

—SAMANTHA CHAPMAN

Your best blush is when flushed.

—AMY ZDUNOWSKI-ROEDER

Target specific goal, monitor, be resolute.

—ARTHUR NINTZEL

Men: daily sex reduces heart disease.

—JACKIE BARTELMO

Mami always said: paper holds everything.

—JULIA ALVAREZ

Write as an artist would paint.

—BRIELLE INTORCIA

Clichés: avoidable in art, *not life*.

—KURT ANDERSEN

Keep your eye on the sleazeballs.

—ANGEL ZAPATA

Invest in a really good haircut.

—*ANNA SCHUMACHER*

Always keep a diaper bag packed.

—*ANNE FEBRAIO MULLINS*

The little joys replace big disappointments.

—*CHANTE ROBERTS*

Failure sows the seeds of success.

—*SEN. MARK WARNER*

Marriage is not 50/50; it's 100/100.

—*ESTHER WOLFE*

Take time to know yourself first.

—*LONNA AMIRA BOWEN*

Vows carelessly spoken are hardly kept.

—JULIUS AGH

Remember to kiss each other goodnight.

—JULIE AGRESTA

Day off, ignore To Do list.

—SARAH DRESSLER

A mistake becomes experience when shared.

—ANGELA FEATHERSTONE

Ask the second question and listen.

—DENISE FRANKLIN TERRY

Priorities change in the emergency room.

—DAN CAMPBELL

Cancer diagnosis really focuses the mind.

—*JOHN CRUTCHER*

Don't ignore that breast lump, sweetie.

—*LEE HUNSAKER*

Seriously, get that mole checked out.

—*MARY ELIZABETH WILLIAMS*

MARRY HAPPILY, LIVE EXTRAVAGANTLY, DIVORCE FRUGALLY.

—*GLENN MYERS*

Spend money on shoes and luggage.

—*DAVID SMALL*

Worry less. Not none; but less.

—*STEVE BODOW*

Say "sorry." Then do it anyway.

—ILIZA SHLESINGER

You are not your neighbor's body.

—RACHEL WEILER

Don't talk behind your own back.

—GALI NETTER

"Next!" Keep it moving for life.

—ALYSSA PINSKER

Ice-cold water: plunge in it weekly.

—ADAM BAER

Not to worry, it's only temporary.

—ARIN FISHKIN

You learn **more** from
your **failures**.

—*PIPER KERMAN*

Right now you're okay, I promise.

—*TAYLOR SCHILLING*

Will it matter in five years?

—*JOYCE CONOVER WELCH*

Capture the atmosphere, capture the moment.

—*COLIN HUGHES*

Don't make life a preemptive strike.

—*BARBARA QUINTILIANO*

Memories look different after forty years.

—*VICTORIA McFEELY*

Always bring a book with you.

—BARBARA DESMOND

Look occupied, they leave you be.

—LUCAS GRAYSON

Procrastination is failure in slow motion.

—BETH LANDERS

There aren't private conversations in crowds.

—BERNIE GOURLEY

Good stories always beat good spreadsheets.

—CHRIS SACCA

Be a kid, even in adulthood.

—CANDACE STEWART

Just have some ice cream already.

—CHRIS HARRIS

Leftover spinach dip makes awesome omelets.

—AMANDA BAUSCH

Hands where I can see 'em.

—GARY SHTEYNGART

Wear heels, wear only those heels.

—AMANDA SCHLEMAN

Always erase the sex tape. Always.

—JOHN ROEDEL

Make love, not war memorial maps.

—BOB SHIFFRAR

Don't let the bastards mold you.

—DEB ALBERTO

Your passions are PARAMOUNT. Pursue them.

—*DAVID HARRIS*

Keep your eyes on the water.

—*BRANDON MEYERS-ORR*

Let crap roll off your back.

—*BRENDA FOSTER*

Learn to swim, not stay afloat.

—*ARIA DING*

Pain is good, alerts to danger.

—*CECILIA BOYLE*

Low expectations make for
impressive accomplishments.

—BRETT ZICARI

Idolize no one, but acknowledge everyone.

—PATRICIA HELBIG

You don't have to marry him.

—BRYANNA BOTHAM

Smile without reason. You'll find one.

—COURTNEY COCCINELLE

Learn **"thank you"** in several languages.

—BEVERLY HEAD

Always take the last flight out.

—PATRICK BELL

Pack extra underwear, you never know.

—SUSAN KATHLEEN TISS

Say YES! Adventure follows, then growth.

—CARLA HALL

Halloween costumes aren't just for kids.

—STEPHANIE GRENDZINSKI

Go to **BURNING MAN** this time.*

—STEPHANIE LOSEE

*She also advises: "Have more sex with more strangers."

Satisfaction is the death to improvement.

—*SARAH SLOBODY*

Karma is justice without the satisfaction.

—*MARCELO MARTINDALE*

Let karma do your dirty work.

—*ARIEL PENN*

You want forgiveness? You must forgive.

—*YVONNE TRACY*

Make bad work. Make it better.

—*DAVID HERSKOVITS*

God doesn't need a plan B.

—*WILLIAM GILMORE*

Make time, take time, give time.

—*MANUELA HERNANDEZ*

Grieve, accept, fight, and push on.

—*DANIELLE GOLDSTEIN*

Put yourself second, but never last.

—*ELISA VAZQUEZ*

Don't push an electric vehicle's range.

—*ED BEGLEY JR.*

Giving up? Give up, give up.

—*UZO ADUBA*

The struggle continues, don't stop now.

—*MELISSA HARRIS-PERRY*

Do not believe your own propaganda.

—NANCY COX DAVIDGE

Lean in always.
        Lean on often.

—*MICHELLE COLLINS*

To learn more, try tougher assignments.

—*LORRIE POTTS*

If it's everyone,
then it's you.

— *CAROLYN HAX*

THE TRUTH IS THE BEST LIE.

—*PARKER REILLY*

Anxiety brews in a lidless pot.

—CAROLINE LEBHERZ

Writing helps to ease the mind.

—CLOE POTTORFF

Just get it off your chest.

—BRYAN PEARSON

Martyrdom is only becoming to saints.

—TERI PORTER

Go outside the building to scream.

—CAROL WILSON

Airing dirty laundry doesn't clean it.

—JONATHAN ZIPPER

Worries vanish temporarily during a workout.

—*PAT MULLIN*

Always stay on your own mat.

—*ANDREA TRIMARCO*

Believe you got the better deal.

—*KITTY MAGUIRE*

Always start with assuming good intentions.

—*TERI EDMAN*

Keep your eye on your luggage.

—*CALVIN TRILLIN*

Except with dynamite, caution is overrated.

—*CAROLINE PAUL*

Disable hot-wire before climbing pasture fence.

—*KATHI WRIGHT*

Don't pee on the electric fence.

—*CATHY BURTON*

Use condoms, look up, read newspapers.

—*CHRISTINA ELLIOTT*

Shiny side up, rubber side down.

—*HEATHER LYNN THOMPSON*

Reading makes you a better writer.

—*MARY-LIZ SHAW*

You need to read more biographies.

—*DONALD BRADLEY*

Read a
classic
novel
every
month.

—*MEAGAN REID-WO*

Allow your true self to change.

—*STEPHEN ELLIOTT*

You'll never win from the middle.

—*LISA JOHNSON*

Go braless as often as possible

—*JO SULLIVAN*

Smile sweetly, then ignore unwarranted advice.

—*MARK BRYANT*

Find your joy in ordinary things.

—*RUTH REICHL*

Play mind games with your hands.

—BARBARA HUCKER

Don't laugh while boss is ranting.

—LESLIE WOLF BRANSCOMB

Dads can make great moms too.

—AHAB PEQUOD

You may decline. No explanations necessary.

—LAURA SIMEON

Remember, french fries are gluten-free.

—RACHEL LAVINE

Stop sharing your dessert: order two.

—LOUIS SMITH

Seek laughter, heartfelt depth, **and pizza**.

—COLLEEN WERTHMANN

Be apart sometimes. Ache with desire.

—PATTY REDLIN

Don't take all the heartaches home.

—T.B. PASQUALE

You've got to marry yourself first.

—CAROLINE WAMPOLE

Don't marry the same man twice.

—NANCY BERGER

Litigate personally, fool for a client.

—RICHARD À BRASSARD

If not documented, it didn't happen.

—LIANA ANGELA

Do the work. Keep the faith.

—RICKY McKINNIE, BLIND BOYS OF ALABAMA

Things that don't matter, shouldn't matter.

—WES MOORE

Ask for help, it's out there.

—NIC SHEFF

No it's not fair. I'm sorry.

—DAVID SHEFF

The concept of God is open-minded.

—AL B. CONAHAN

DON'T tell me what I think.

—*FLASH ROSENBERG*

DON'T believe a word I say.

—*TRICIA BOCZKOWSKI*

Thin line between balls and stupidity.

—*VINNIE OAKES*

Thou shalt not yell "Freebird." *Ever.*

—*ANDY LANGER*

Saying "be creative" squashes creative bug.

—*KATHERINE KENNEDY*

Always be each other's best editors.

—*DAN JONES*

Chances are, your editor is right.

—ELIZABETH GILBERT

Dream big and don't fear erasers.

—BETH CARTER

Don't worry who gets the credit.

—KEITH JACKSON

Lighten your load: let grudges go.

—ELLIOTT HOLT

Loss accepted is loss less painful.

—MARIE PAQUET-NESSON

Meditation: as misunderstood as bull terriers.

—*DANIELLE CLARO*

Sometimes blind trust is good enough.

—*ANYA HUNTER*

In pithy situations, resort to haiku.

—*ZEPHERIN AYCE*

A haiku is not a koan.

—*ALLEN PETERSON*

You probably already know the answer.

—*YAEL ROBERTS*

Wanna be loved?
GET A DOG.
—*CAMRON ASSADI*

Having a baby?
GET A DOG.
—*HEIDI WAGNER MacLAREN*

Admit your failings and make amends.

—ANNE BROWN

Stop looking for someone to blame.

—DAVID ALEXANDER S. DIAL

Failure? An event. Not a person.

—JOHN TSILIMPARIS

Try not to be an asshole.

—DAVID WOLKIN

Take a shower. You'll feel better.

—DAWN R. DUGLE

Laughter is necessary,
                 yelling is not.

—*DANDA LYON*

No laughter in the office? LEAVE.

—*MICHELE REZNIK*

Never confuse a memo with reality.

—*KEITH HERRMANN*

Let photography be your second language.

—*MARGARITA MAVROMACHLIS*

People, like photos, can be cropped.

—*LINDSEY ROTH-ROSEN*

Never try to hide your freckles.

—GAIL HUGGARD

Being underestimated is a marvelous weapon.

—DIANNA MASSEY

Your thumb goes outside your fist.

—DESTINY COLLIER

Remember the echo, it does return.

—DIANNE ZEIGLER

Strong women have equally strong handshakes.

—LINDSAY BERRA

Hold hands and hold your tongue.

—*DYAN TITCHNELL*

Caring touch heals deep wounds sweetly.

—*JENNIFER PLIEGO*

When in doubt, administer extravagant self-care.

—*SUZANNE CLORES*

Without trust, it's not really love.

—KELLIE FOURNIER

Let the kids see you kissing.

—DEAN EVANS

Don't be cheap. Buy the flowers.

—JAMEYLEE NUSS

Get a partner, not a backpack.

—GRACE MARIE DRUPALS

You get what you settle for.

—DEBORAH WILLIAMS

Don't text. Write a love letter.

—ELISA SHEVITZ

Just keep on saying good morning.

—EDWINA JOY AKENS

Smile at all the mean kids.

—ELENA ELDER

With crowns and fillings, don't economize.

—GAIL HART

Smile while you still have teeth.

—ABBEY PLAYLE

Don't lose your security badge. **Ever**.

—MAIA KAYSER

Toys are for children, not desks.

—BRYONY PUNT

Buy goldfish, which die, as lessons.

—BEN GREENMAN

Early worm gets eaten by bird.

—BETH LISICK

Madness takes toll; have exact change.

—CHARLIE WOLF

Mom's crazy. Get used to it.

—ELLEN MILBOURN

Torch your bridges, explore your path.

—JOSHIE ARMSTEAD

Do not do routine things routinely.

—EMILIE STAAT

Gather newspaper clippings.
Discard newspaper clippings.

—EMILY SPIVACK

Your past is not your future.

—EMILY CUMMING

Nothing fills jagged holes just right.

—ELLIS REYES

If it feels hollow, it is.

—LIZETTE QUESADA PEREZ

Find where walls can come down.

—AILYN SIERPE

Measure twice, cut once, regret less.

—REBECCA KLEIN

Make more with your short sticks.

—LUCIE SMOKER

A stiff prick knows no conscience.

—ANDY GOODMAN

"Tequila Time!" brings a family together.

—*FELIZIA NAVA-KARDON*

Laced with tequila, thoughts turn poetic.

—*DANIEL L. SHIELDS*

Do age *gracefully* and also *gratefully*.

—*ANNA WATSON*

Love letters saved comfort old age.

—*PATTI PILEGGI*

You will grow hair almost everywhere.

—*TERRY BAIN*

Everyone's just as clueless as YOU.

—ELIZABETH ASHLEY CROWDER

Starting point of achievement is desire.

—MATT PRATHER

Picture books tame first grader beasts.

—GABRIEL ROSENBERG

The smell of vomit eventually fades.

—GABRIELLA DIFILLIPPO

Don't be ashamed of your scars.

—*VANDANA WALIA*

The blade is never the answer.

—*HANNAH E. REED*

Study Strunk and White. Consult Roget's.

—*JANE STILLINGER*

"It's" equals "it is." Otherwise, "its."

—*DAN ROLLMAN*

The plural of "fish" is "fish."

—*RONDA ALEXANDER*

Danger! Never rely solely on spellcheck!

—*JAYNE McKENZIE*

Always check Urban Dictionary before repeating.

—*ABBY LULL*

Listen listen listen listen . . . then talk.

—*JJ RAMBERG*

Give. Give. Give more. Get. Give. . . .

—*SAM KAUFFMAN*

Writing is like sex; be sincere.

—*GOPALA KRISHNAN*

A good example always trumps advice.

—*WAYNE SCHEER*

Wait 24 hours before hitting "send."

—CRAIG KANARICK

Emails remember facts better than participants.

—JEFF HARRIS

New rule: no email before coffee.

—MARTINE ZILVERSMIT

Texting while walking is dangerous too.

—AMY LAUREN

Don't keep secrets in the cloud.

—PAUL BECKMAN

No bananas in your still life.

—*SUSAN WINSLOW*

Eat a banana after a workout.

—*EUN-JEE RHEE*

Out of shampoo? Use beer instead.

—*EMILI RUDBECK*

YES! Vinegar water = streakless clean!

—*CHRISTINA VRBA*

Lemons smell better and clean immaculately.

—*DANA SHAW*

Banana skins ease mosquito bite itch.

—*CHRISTINE BENSON*

Rubbing alcohol always removes permanent marker.

—*ANAMARIE GUNDERSEN*

"Pickle" is both noun and verb.

—*RICK FIELD*

Don't be so afraid to tell.

—*JOANIE JARRETT*

There's no shame in starting over.

—*GREG CONWAY*

With Duct-tape, you can MacGyver anything.

—*BUFFY KINSTLE*

Wet firewood lights if it's cured.

—*TOM MAXWELL*

You should never force anything mechanical.

—*MARCI GURTON*

Anything's possible with an extension cord.

—*BILLY KELLER*

Sleep when the baby is sleeping.

—*CHRIS AMICK*

Baby doesn't know you are inexperienced.

—*MARY JANE BILYK*

Catch falls, catch hugs, catch naps.

—*SUSAN EVIND*

Never date men prettier than you.

—*HEATHER HANLON NICHOLS*

Marry someone smarter than you are.

—*HELEN LAMBERTH*

Remember why you fell in love.

—*ANNIS CASSELLS*

Mistakes made young better your life.

—*HELEN RAMSEY*

#Dude! #Don't #use #so #many #hashtags!

—HARUKI WAKAMATSU

Share thy Wi-Fi password with guests.

—KYLE WRATHER

Vent in Word, not in email.

—INGELIS JENSEN

Mind your own damn business already.

—JAMES GANDY

Walking: guaranteed to foil slow metabolism.

—KRISTEN GRIMM

Tin hats, guaranteed to foil aliens.

—DAVID DREHER

Sometimes cyber relationships are much easier.

—*JERILYNN KARR*

Always ask for a recent picture.

—*BRET THOMAS*

Find the bars they drink in.

—*RORY O'CONNOR*

Flirt shamelessly and get free drinks.

—*KATE DELUCA*

Managers are judged above and below.

—JOHN REILLY

You can't hide a piggyback ride.

—JASON ADAMS

Do not mistake function for form.

—J. PATRICK BENNETT

Your trophies will be good storytellers.

—MIKE HELTON

The job doesn't love you back.

—JANET HUBER BELLOWS

Be the teacher you would want.

—*MARIE BOLLERS*

Teaching will test your improvisational abilities.

—*EASTER DODDS*

Teach me to remember. Not cram.

—*JACOB GOODIN*

Yoga: hold the pose, good-bye woes.

—*LESLEY GRINBERG*

Dance like drunk people at weddings.

—*JAMES SEELY*

Let go lest you be dragged.

—*JENNY GIVLER KOCH*

Time's static. We're the ones going.

—*CHRISTOPHER McNEILL*

Don't waste your rarity or clarity.

—*KRISTOPHER MALLORY*

Positive energy flow: successful interior design.

—*MAGGIE BLAU*

Food tastes better in remodeled kitchens.

—*BETH BATES*

Renovations are for the mentally insane.

—*JEANETTE CHEEZUM*

Home remodel? Hire contractor, marriage counselor.

—*MOLLY DITMORE*

Life's too short for IKEA construction.

—*JACI STEPHEN*

Only the delusional get things done.

—ISABEL TOWNSEND-LAST

Splurge for maid service and relax.

—NANCY LaPARO

Everyone isn't going to like you.

—JOAN STAMM

You're a troublemaker. Keep it up.

—JESSICA NASTAL-DEMA

Learn your lines; trust your audience.

—SARAH JONES

Never follow a script; write it.

—JULIA ARMET

End the scene with a BANG.

—COURTNEY KEMP AGBOH

Write once. Revise twice. Revise twice.

—BARBARA J STARMANS

Proofread: ensure you didn't anything out.

—JOSIE CANNELLA

Trust your gut, shape your butt.

—SARA BLAKELY

You learn more by keepin' quiet.

—JAMES "SON" THOMAS

Two ears, one mouth. Use proportionately.

—JOE McGUIRE

When you tell a story, listen.

—DAVID JOE MILLER

Your mask first, then the child's.

—JULIA HICKS DE PEYSTER

Be the someone they can call.

—NATALIE JAY

You get older;
Dad becomes smarter.

—*JOEL RIMBY*

Mom and Dad always know best.

—*LAURA LeGRAND*

Never live on anyone else's timetable.

—*KAYLA BRUNER*

High school will be irrelevant, someday.

—*PAIGE VERMEER*

When cookies are passed, **take one**.

—MARY ANN VECCHIONE

Pee at each and every opportunity.

—JOHN CALDWELL

Never pass up a clean bathroom.

—LOIS ALTER MARK

Do not ever threaten to quit.

—PAT GRUBE

Quitting may just be the answer.

— LAIPENG SPAGNOLETTI

Begin as you mean to proceed.

—*JUDY MITCHELL WERNER*

Write your eulogy. Make it true.

—*JONATHAN SJORDAL*

Prevention is the most effective cure.

—*ANDREA MARIA SIPIN*

Never trust a fart while juicing.

—*JULIE SWEUM*

Beware the instruction of sex-starved gurus.

—*KELLY BODOH*

Intercourse is easy.
Discourse is hard.

—*ABBY ELLIN*

Nothing matters more than the truth.

—DAVID KIRBY

Take your time. It goes fast.

—SUSAN ORLEAN

Speeding doesn't turn the clock back.

—KAREN BENNETT

Drive like nobody else knows how.

—MARTHA JOHNSON

They're called turn signals. Use them.

—VANIDIE SNOWDEN

Sociopaths make poor business partners, spouses.

—BECKY RIDER

Anger does not change the facts.

—*KATHERINE BOLINGER*

Never pluck your eyebrows when angry!

—*KELLI PETERSON ARREDONDO*

When angry, just count to six.

—*ANTTI AUTIO*

ANGER MANAGEMENT:
get a drum set.

—*JACE DANIEL*

It's okay. Go to bed angry.

—JULIE BELLOMO GWIASDA

You can always use more sleep.

—DAN LEWIS

Befriend insomnia and enjoy the night.

—MARIA RENGERS

Emptiest subway car: not your friend.

—MARY GRYGIEL

TV remote isn't an isolation device.

—*WILL GOURLEY*

THE INTERNET IS NOT YOUR FRIEND.

—*KELLY KRETH*

Everyone suffers from chronic email syndrome.

—*M. C. NICHOLSON*

Your inbox will never be empty.

—*NANCY ADAMS*

Don't open more than five tabs.

—*DANIEL GOLDMAN*

The "save" button is your friend.

—*GILLIAN RAMOS*

Count vacation days, not sick days.

—ELIZABETH KALMAN

Take the trip you promised yourself.

—KRISTYN WASHBURN

Always buy lemonade from the kids.

—GREGORY PAYNE

Sign the card. Eat the cake.

—KEVIN KUNREUTHER

Note to selfie: keep chin down.

—JOSEPHINE COLLETT

Don't let your things control you.

—LAURA CATTANO

Better to disgrace than to bore.

—*JACK DOWNING*

Practice being bored. It builds character.

—*LAUREN LIPTON*

Always look behind you when gossiping.

—*JUDY AMSTERDAM*

Do not gossip while I'm gossiping.

—*LAURIE-ANNE LÉVESQUE*

A baby doesn't die from crying.

—*VERONICA RICHARDSON*

No child
      starves to death quietly.

—*REBECCA ANN MAHURIN*

No child
      grows by being measured.

—*LINDA ERSKINE*

Do something for someone worse off.

—*LINDSAY BROOKE*

Aesthetically pleasing does not mean beauty.

—*SARAH BROOKS*

DO NO HARM, TAKE NO SHIT.

—*LISA ANN GALLAGHER*

Find a maestro; ask them questions.

—*KATHERINE CAMPBELL*

Know security guards, cleaners by name.

—*WESLEY COLL*

Don't look down, you might stumble.

—*LUKE WESTERVELT*

Helpful and helpless are thin lines.

—*JENA KRUMRINE*

Speak in shorter sentences than this.

—*LYNN CROXTON*

Delete almost all adjectives and adverbs.

—*LYNN HARRIS*

See the world; savor the differences.

—*LYNNE WEINBERGER*

Decisions open doors, decisions close doors.

—*LYNSEY STEWART*

Never trust gentlemen with pinky rings.

—*SARAH BATES JOHNSON*

Laugh at yourself every DAMN day.

—*OPHIRA EISENBERG*

You don't always need to win.

—MELISSA MASOOM

Try to remember the first hello.

—KATSUHIKO KINOSHITA

You're not learning when you're speaking.

—MILAGROS VEGA

Admit mistakes. You'll be respected more.

—KRYSTYNA FEDOSEJEVS

Let toddler take you for walk.

—DEBORAH A. CUNEFARE

Always play, always explore, always love.

—*LAURIE RICHARDS*

Never forget, love is a verb.

—*ALISON ADAMS PERLAC*

Aim high, strive hard, be humble.

—*AMY CHUA*

Buy candy your kids don't like.

—*TOBY MANEWITH*

Always share your cookies with me.

—*LISA DICKEY*

Seat yourself at the grown-up table.

—*RACHEL FERSHLEISER*

Cheese and crackers IS a meal.

—*CANDACE HILL*

If all else fails, eat biscuits.

—*KIRAN FLIP SINGH SIRAH*

Paint what is in your backyard.

—*MARY HAGY*

Run with kites, not with scissors.

—*MARY PAT HYLAND*

NOBODY, NOBODY KNOWS WHAT
THEY'RE DOING.*

—DANIEL HANDLER

*His alter ego, Lemony Snicket, advises:
"Never, ever refuse a breath mint."

Wake up. Be awesome. Sleep. Repeat.

—MATT DiGERONIMO

PLAY, PLAY, PLAY, PLAY, PLAY, **PLAY**.

—L. G. SMITH

Act to impress yourself before others.

—MARZIA NERI

Don't close ears for hard advice.

—MATTHEW BURGOS

Don't just hear, make yourself listen.

—MATT WEISHER

To thine own self be glue.

—MATT REGAN

Love them while you have them.

—DONNA RITCHIE

Press EVERY button until printer works.

—MELESHA OWEN

Pack black. Be done with it.

—HEATHER POOLE

iPhone to identify pills when hospitalized.

—DONNA HARING

DON'T LOOK UP AT BIRDS FLYING.

—TAMMIE PATTON

Never play leapfrog with a unicorn.

—MELISSA SIMON

Don't mess with a mother hen.

—TERESA CANTER

On holidays, avoid wet kissing aunts.

—CHRISTINA DELIA

Not everything has to be fixed.

—MICHELLE SMITH

Find someone who laughs a lot.

—MIGS MARFORI

Listen to the uncles. They know.

—MICHAEL CALLAHAN

When in doubt, make it funky.

—McKENZIE MERRIMAN

Anger simply takes too much energy.

—MOLLY BAIR

Your rage will eventually devour you.

—EMMA WOLFIN GOLDING

Only stay angry for fifteen minutes.

—JENNIFER BAIR

Trust your outrage. Turn to wonder.

—COURTNEY MARTIN

Kindness is never wasted, or forgotten.

—BRIGITTE PETERSON

Spend more on **shoes** than **clothes**.

—*GAIL KAISER*

Persistence has more value than qualifications.

—*MITCH POLACK*

Don't let your degree define you.

—*KELLY HEANEY*

It's not too late for college.

—*MIKE WHITNEY*

Beware, sometimes later can become never.

—*AUMA OBAMA*

It's never too late for Paris.

—*MARIA LEOPOLDO*

Avoid the drama. Sign contracts upfront.

—NICOLA BEHRMAN

Dear younger self: start saving money.

—NEESHA HOSEIN

Don't ever wish to be older.

—MARIE WOLF

Don't hunt happiness; the hunted run.

—EUGENE PAULISH

Count your blessings, not your problems.

—NICOLA JANE WILLETTS

Half empty? Perhaps a smaller glass.

—*ELLEN HERD*

Don't ignore all those red flags.

—*ANGEL SEMAILIS*

If you hit her, you've lost.

—*CINDY POULIN*

See something bad? Do something good.

—*DONNA LOWE*

Hear your silent screams and act.

—*RUTH MACBEAN*

Let childhood horrors breed compassionate hearts.

—*JOAN HEYDEN*

Supply your own compass and rudder.

—*KITTY MAGUIRE*

You're an adult. *Get over it.*

—*LAURA FRASER*

With good hair, anything is possible.

—*KAREN GOLDEN*

Treat infants like terrorists: no negotiating.

—ZOE ALLEN

Don't baby them after they're babies.

—CAMILLE SWEENEY

Raising them means letting them go.

—O. D. LUMP

Do not make my mistakes yours.

—ALY RINEHART

Parents did their part. **Do yours**.

—KIM GAMBLE

Introduce children to your inner child.

—JO ANN DANIELS

Learn these two words: "Yes, Dear."

—PAT CLEVENGER

Speeches sink or swim with emotion.

—PETE PANTELIDAKIS

A promise is done, not said.

—PAUL BACHMANN

Always laugh at your father's jokes.

—SANDI MARX

Explain the questions your dad avoided.

—PAUL HARRINGTON

Your dad will be your hero.

—SUZANNE WORRELL

Stay in bed, read a book.

—*NANCY KENT*

So many dead writers to read.

—*VENDELA VIDA*

Read great books, not good ones.

—*PAUL LEROUX*

Read Shakespeare! He said it all.

—*RICHARD M. JOHNSON*

Nine foot board, three foot wave.

—PETER CAVANAGH

Battle the lows, **ride the highs.**

—ALAYNA MAE BATES

GIVING CRITICISM: positive, negative, positive sandwich.

—OLIVIA ARRINGTON

Never start with, "No offense, but . . ."

—POLLY MATH

Good manners are always in style.

—PEGGY POST

Thou shall not post sharing threats.

—SHERYL CLOUD

Considering children?
Decide before time does.

—RACHEL LEHMANN-HAUPT

It's okay not to have kids.

—SIMA WALKER

Careful what you say to siblings.

—JACOB FORSTER ROTHBART, AGE 8

Your cat: don't stand on her.

— *NATALIE FORSTER ROTHBART, AGE 3*

Never fondle your pregnant wife's breasts.

— *MICHAEL FORSTER ROTHBART*

Hit the road, talk to strangers.

— *DAVY ROTHBART*

Meditation is
e x p a n s i v e   s p a c i o u s n e s s
opening daily.

— *BARBARA BRODSKY ROTHBART*

A thing of beauty lasts forever.

— *HAL ROTHBART*

Brain is useless without lunch breaks.

—ROBIN PARAISO

Vacations are meant to be taken.

—ANTONIA MARIE KELLY

Leave your comfort zone at home.

—RICHARD GUSTMAN

Never underestimate the power of stupidity.

—OLIVIA WEBB

Never eat where dumpster is full.

—LYNN LeBLANC

Don't be afraid to be young.

—*PAIGE CANO*

Youth is not an age range.

—*RYAN NOEL*

Don't play the other guy's game.

—*ALLAN BENTON*

Life expires without an expiration label.

—*MARGARET ADAMS*

SECRET OF LIFE:

family, friends, bacon.

—*KATIE COURIC*

don't impress everybody.

—*JESSICA ERDMAN*

write your story.

—*MARC BRYANT*

marry an Italian.

—*NORA EPHRON*

Never fake
orgasms,
laughter,
or death.

—REGINA BARRECA

Don't stick that in your ear.

—*LAEL WEYENBERG*

Don't nibble at life. Bite hard.

—*RUTH LIVINGSTONE*

Fly fearlessly, regret nothing you love.

—*ERICA JONG*

It's good to be untamed sometimes.

—*KIMBERLY ROSE SMITH*

Be yourself and success will follow.

—*BILL PHILLIPS*

Not everyone can be Batman. Yet.

—*SEAN RAMESWARAM*

Truth never fails to come through.

—*STEPHANIE SNYDER*

Let it go. Make up now.

—*TERRY MOLINARI*

Debate to learn, not to win.

—SCARLET FUENTES

Truth is always in the middle.

—TERRI BELL

Lose your temper, lose your case.

—SHERRY BEER

Know when to cut and run.

—SALLY LARSON

All rules have exceptions (even this).

—DAN BROOK

Your only constant companion is yourself.

—NICHOLE ARGYRES

Show up. You can sleep later.

—FELICIA ALLEY

Never marry the dumb cute one.

—*SHEILA ROSE MONTGOMERY*

Boys don't just look for personality.

—*JAMIE MANVILLE*

Don't wait three days to call.

—*SASCHA ROTHCHILD*

Both let down your guard together.

—*LISA CLARK*

Don't take your spouse for granted.

—*SIMA WALKER*

Don't forget to cc your spouse.

—*ANDY GREENE*

Don't tell your husband's lover's husband.

—*EMELINE LAI*

Always beware the "reply all" button.

—*BRIAN STING*

Life is better in soft pajamas.

—*EMILY CULBERTSON*

Always get your bra properly fitted.

—*SAMM COLLINS*

Self-respect comes in plus size too.

—*MEGHAN HOSKINS*

Laughter is good for the abs.

—*JOY BAILEY*

If it frightens you? Do it.

—*AMANDA PALMER*

Pay attention to that gnawing feeling.

—*SUSAN VARNEY SPEIER*

If it feels wrong, it is.

—*SABRINA CRUZ-MUNOZ*

Assumptions are the
mother of f**k-ups.

—*SALLY EVERETT*

Message to parents: **pick your battles**.

—ROZ CHAST

Every now and then wear plaid.

—ANN MOCCHI

Watch out. Kids can smell fear.

—SHAYAL VASHISTH

Allow children their own life plan.

—MANDIP KAUR SANDHER

Secret to relationships: excellent oral skills.

—*ERIC KALMAN*

Parents, friends: finitude is for real.

—*CHARLES C. MANN*

You need to RESPECT your boundaries.

—*DANIEL GAZTAMBIDE*

Try not to finish people's sentences.

—*LEIGH GIZA*

People are the experts on themselves.

—*HEATHER GOLD*

Anticipatory anxiety? Don't look, just leap.

—ELLEN HENDRIKSEN

Anxiety management tip:
expect logical outcomes.

—SAUMYA GANGULY

Don't lose your mind, lasso it.

—MARIE PATIENCE

Dance when your tires are deflated.

—RACHEL N. SPEAR

Purpose and passion equals your destiny.

—SUNNY HOSTIN

Pursue what makes you **COME ALIVE**.

—MARI MITCHELL

Break the velvet handcuffs. Live again.

—DAVID RHODES

Live your values. At work too.

—LAURA SCHER

You get paid for the disappointment.

—CHUCK KLOSTERMAN

You embarrass yourself when you lie.

—*AARON KRISH*

Work a little harder and watch.

—*COLIN WALSH*

Break everything down into baby steps.

—*VIVIAN CHUM*

Mental note: actual notes are better.

—*LEE WALSH*

Don't hold grudges. Life's too long.

—*BRIAN SPELLMAN*

Always write a thank you note.

—ALEXANDRA LANGE

Thank you cards get you hired.

—KIMBERLY SHERRELL

Today's coworker could be tomorrow's boss.

—DANETTE HOFFERT

Bacon pineapple pizza with chipotle tobacco.

—JASON BITNER

Always write your next job description.

—MARY BUIKEMA

Teamwork is overestimated. Delegation is not.

—SIMON DE CASTRO

Never, ever hog all the bed.

—HEATHER SHARPE

Always keep one foot in workforce.

—STACEY REISS

Don't let friends drink and blog.

—LISA CARLSON

Someone at work reads your blog.

—AMANDA GREEN

Finish one book, pick up another.

—DANA PERROW MORAN

Find love and lessons **in bookstores**.

—AUTUMN WISE

Life can grind. Make daily blend.

—CHRIS KILLIP

Second cup of coffee: results unpredictable.

—AMIEE BLAISDELL

Don't fight people in Facebook comments.

—*CHELSEY DRYSDALE*

Keep your family drama off Facebook.

—*PATRICIA HENDERSON*

Do not Facebook stalk old crushes.

—*LACY FOLAND*

Don't ever push a "mystery" button.

—*DEBERA GATLINI TOWNLINI*

If you have to ask, no.

—*STEVEN WOLFE*

All dogs think they are lapdogs.

—STEPH ROSE

Check behind shower curtain for cats.

—DONNA TALARICO

Orphans and songs deserve good homes.

—SHERRILL BLACKMAN

Pay attention to Bob Dylan's lyrics.

—STACY MEYROWITZ

Grab a guitar. Learn to play.

—STEPHANIE HANSEN

Listen to more Willie Nelson songs.

—KATHERINE CAVALIERE

You can write your own song.

—JASON BURLESON, ROB ICKES, SHAWN LANE, TIM STAFFORD, WAYNE TAYLOR, AKA BLUE HIGHWAY

Go ahead, serve your country. Anywhere!

—*JJ JAY*

Engage in something BIGGER than yourself.

—*MARY CRESCENZO*

Courage is contagious, so is cowardice.

—*CHAD GRACE*

Fear isn't a safe hiding place.

—*KAITLYNN HOLEWA*

ON DEATH: have an exit strategy.

—GEORGE SOSA

Can't move wall? **Turn. Face room**.

—LISA FOGEL

Many ways in, one way out.

—PATRICK MOLONEY

Live life to the half fullest!

—GOPAL KAMAT

Life is magical, but not Disney-magical.

—LESLIE HOBSON

Always practice coming back to love.

—*TAYLOR HARKNESS*

Humor cuts through thoughts of heartbreak.

—*SEAN SNARR-JONES*

Detach from cerebral, act from heart.

—*TINA BIEDRONSKI*

Don't let heartbreak make you hard.

—*AMBER HALL*

Forsan et hæc olim meminisse juvabit.*

—*DAVID RHODY*

*"Someday even this may be a good memory,"
a Latin teacher's translation of a passage from *The Aeneid*

Bend and lift with your legs.

—*TIM HEARD*

Structure and flexibility in equal measure.

—*IAN SAGITTARIAN*

Healing is hard, but obstinacy kills.

—*HOLLAND PRIOR*

Accept change. You might need it.

—*SARAH FORD*

Make mistakes, else you're making mistakes.

—*AL FILREIS*

Even tiny mutations make big changes.

—*ELERI HAMILTON*

Write it pretty—only dumbasses mind.

—*RICK BRAGG*

The sun will always come again.

—*ADINA JONKE*

Choose not to take it personally.

—*ALEX LESMAN*

Thoughts become things. Think good thoughts.

—*PAUL DALAL*

Love thy neighbors, even thy idiots.

—*LAURA DERRINGTON*

Don't bark back at barking dogs.

—*SANJIDA SHAHEED*

Magic 8-ball makes the best decisions.

—*JENNIFER KENNINGTON*

Be good. Have fun. Bring mace.

—*SHIRA GINSBURG*

Walk quickly and wear loud clothes.

—*BETH LYNN CARDALL LEEHY*

Cleaning, cooking . . . it all can wait.

—*SANDRA RAUB*

Everything you do is your signature.

—*ROBERT THOMPSON*

Always be yourself. Unless you stink.

—*RANDI BARNES*

Okay. Let me think on that.

—ZEV BOROW

Red wine: best sipped slightly chilled.

—ANTHONY GIGLIO

Life's too short for cheap cigars.

—CHRISTOPHER JOHNSON

Drink expensive champagne when celebrating life!

—TIFFANY CHESNOSKY

Desire the perfect; love the imperfect.

—SCOTT J. WILSON

Between two sleeping dogs is heaven.

—*MANDY STADTMILLER*

Little and often fills the purse.

—*TERRI KITCHENS SONNENBURG*

Never borrow money from a friend.

—*TINA MORTIMER*

Don't loan things you care about.

—*REBECCA STADOLNIK*

Borrower is slave to the lender.

—*CANDEE HOWELL BRAKEFIELD*

Call your family without wanting money.

—*MELANIE DELORME*

Just lend your brother the money.

—*ANDRE GOLUBIC*

Going through hell? **Ask for directions**.

—*RACHAEL SOLOMON*

When in doubt, find another route.

—*KEVORK MAHSEREJIAN*

DON'T WAIT YOUR TURN IN LIFE.

—*MICHAEL FABIANO*

The zen of the right lane.

—CATHY ALTER

True wisdom: know you know nothing.

—JENNIFER JENNINGS

God's in charge—don't mess up.

—JEAN MERRIMAN

Always stay in the Pleasant Tense.

—FRANK TENNYSON

Write Six to diminish neurological decline.

—JIM RALEIGH

WRITE A SIX, THEN A CHAPTER.

—DICK PETERSON

Spread whatever joy you can muster.

—SCOTT STEIN

Edit your words, not your dreams.

—SUSAN BREEDEN

First draft revision? Just paper cuts.

—DAMION MEYER

Remember that all advice is autobiographical.

—BEN GUTTMANN

Do **not** ask me for advice.

—TOM PERROTTA

This may all be a simulation.

—DAVID EAGLEMAN

What's written now means more later.

—JOHN SIMONDS

Look back, but don't ever stare.

—KAHRA BUSS

Take some time to not think.

—EPIPHANY JONES

If in doubt the answer's "**Yes**."

—*MICHAEL FINKEL*

Offer your help, not your advice.

—*DAVID ROTH*

Never give advice to a stranger.

—*JOANNA WESTON*

It's all about **entrances** and **exits**.

—*KATHERINE WESSLING*

Remember that endings can be beautiful.

—*KAYLA CURL*

Can't say something nice? Try fiction.

—*DAVID BALDACCI*

Don't read the last chapter first.

—ERIC SIMONOFF

Acknowledgments

"The trick is to be grateful," David Carr reminds us at the end of his own memoir. Those six words from the late writer and mentor to many offer a sentiment I try to remind myself of each day. There are so many people who have made the Six-Word Memoir® project shine. My former editor at SMITH Magazine and coeditor of the first four six-word books, Rachel Fershleiser, created and nourished this project with me from its inception. I'd like to thank my associate editor Shauna Healy Greene for her invaluable work in every part of the creation of this book. More than six words of appreciation goes out to community manager, Jonathan Zipper, interns Caroline Goldstein, Allison Volpe, and McKenzie Merriman, and "poweruser" Laureatte Loy, who knows many words but not "no" when she is seeking six-word stories from others. Daniela Rapp and her team at St. Martin's Press have been a joy to work with as we put together a puzzle with many, many pieces, as has my agent and friend, David Patterson. My wife, Piper, is my editor, ear, and nonstop source of care and counsel in every part of my life. Our little boy's love of language reminds me why I do what I do each and every day.

Index

About the Author

Larry Smith is the founder and editor of SMITH Magazine, home of the Six-Word Memoir® project, which has become a bestselling series of seven books, a board game, live event series, and a global phenomenon that's inspired people of all ages across the world. Larry speaks on the power of storytelling at companies such as ESPN, Levi's, and Google, as well as nonprofits, foundations, and schools across the country.

One Life. Six Words. What's Yours?™

Since the Six-Word Memoir® made its debut in 2006, more than one million short life stories have been shared on the storytelling community SMITH Magazine. In classrooms and boardrooms, churches and synagogues, veterans' groups and across the dinner table, Six-Word Memoirs have become a powerful tool to catalyze conversation, spark imagination, or simply break the ice.

Share a Six-Word Memoir on any part of your life at

www.sixwordmemoirs.com.